The Compiled Work
Barrie Cooke Boo
(& families literature le

1925 – 2011
Book 2

Published and Book design by
Stephen Cooke

Revision 1.0

ISBN: 9798607952686

FOREWARD

Following on from Barrie's first book of compiled poems, this book contains his remaining short works, poems and written accounts of the family history. read them carefully, understand their meaning and you will understand this truly inspirational gentleman. I am very proud to be able to bring this book to publication and endurance through time.

These poems contain the insight of an intelligent and brilliant imagination, a fighter and loyal husband who enjoyed his writing and wrote many times about the RAF and his time during the war years, which eventually lead to him writing his first book about an abandoned military camp... So they thought. Politics were another strong aspect of his upbringing with ties to family members within parliament such as the legendary Crawshay Bailey, an industrialist and elected MP who became one of the great iron-masters of wales. Most of all, and close to all our hearts were his shorts about family, friends and the sights and sounds of childhood. I hope you love this book, the inspirational and inspiring messages, with maybe a little bit of humour here and there!

Taken from : 'To Ann Harper in response to a letter from Australia'

As a nation we're a failure,
And things have reached a pretty pass,
When told by people in Australia,
To wipe our bums with tufts of grass.

This Book also contains the remaining poems and shorts I was left by Vicky (My grandma) written by Barrie and other family members, from there sons, grandsons and granddaughters, friends and past family members. Later in the book the poems and writing are mostly by my Great Grandmother Nan Ramsey, the foundations on which Barrie and Vicki grew to become who they were.

All these poems were left in the safe keeping of Vicki and then passed to me at the time of her passing. I promised this literature would not be forgotten and I would publish it. All photograph's are from the family collection.

All Rights Reserved ©StephenCCooke(2020)

In Loving Memory

CONTENTS

A little family History

Page   7, Just a little family history
Page   9, Memories of Shanklin
Page   10, The Connatty's
Page   10, Memories

The Home, Friends & Family

Page   13, Thoughts of Home
Page   19, To my darling wife... Thank you for my son, David
Page   33, My Best Friends
Page   34, Absent Friends
Page   35, When Jackie Married Grahame (1973)
Page   49, Addendum to the above
Page   49, a forlorn hope
Page   51, Mother's day
Page   53, When David played for England against wales
Page   54, Laura
Page   55, Odes to mum when she's away. 'till then.
Page   56, An ode for recovery. By David Cooke
Page   56, Is A Puzzlement!
Page   56, Welcome Home – er darling
Page   57, Get well soon - You 'orrible little patient you
Page   58, Miss You
Page   59, Missing you
Page   60, Ode to one with Laryngitis
Page   61, To Vicki
Page   62, To David and Jill on there Wedding day.
Page   63, Odes to mum's maths
Page   67, Dad!!
Page   68, The Washing up Blues
Page   68, Another Welcome Home
Page   69, Lynette
Page   70, To Mum and Dad Cooke with Love
Page   71, To a very Special Grandmother
Page   73, The Naughty Thirty Six (1945)

Page	74, Father's Lament
Page	75, Missing You
Page	76, Alone
Page	78, Mother's Day Poem from Mark to his Mom
Page	78, Nan
Page	79, Life Sometimes
Page	80, A Sad/Glad Story
Page	81, From Frank to Monica on there 50th Anniversary
Page	82, A poem from me to you
Page	82, Disillusion
Page	85, For eve and Doug on there fiftieth Wedding Anniversary
Page	85, Mother's day poem from Mark to his Mum
Page	87, David left his Razor Behind
Page	89, Observing the Tye
Page	89, Blessings
Page	90, My Life
Page	90, My grandsons
Page	91, My Eighteenth Birthday
Page	91, Thoughts on a Lovely Daughter
Page	92, Looking Back
Page	92, A comfort to both Mum and Dad
Page	93, Yesterday's Rugby Match
Page	93, To Vicki and Barrie on there 25th Wedding Anniversary
Page	93, David Cooke
Page	94, Twenty Three on the Tenth
Page	94, A new Generation
Page	95, Nest day, Called – I Dust
Page	95, Vicki's 47th Birthday
Page	95, Vicki's 45th Birthday
Page	96, Barrie
Page	96, David! Twenty Ninth Birthday
Page	96, Chris and his Guitar
Page	97, Grahame and his sons
Page	97, Happy Birthday Alex
Page	98, Happy Official Birthday Alex
Page	98, Vicki
Page	98, To Commemorate Bobby's Birth
Page	99, Vicki's Birthday 24/3/1978
Page	99, Christopher's Day 1978

In Loving Memory

Page	99, Vicki's Birthday 24/3/80
Page	100, Birthday Poem 24/3/1926
Page	100, A Birthday Poem to Vicky Written over two Days 24/3/76
Page	100, From Gwen Tester July 2002
Page	101, From Mark 4th October 2003
Page	101, The Blessing
Page	104, A poem from David
Page	103, Dad
Page	104, Grandad
Page	11, Ode to an Ode-Maker
Page	12, Edith
Page	84, To Mum and Dad

The World War

Page	14, Boyhood Memories
Page	16, A Tribute to the RAF (Written in 1943)
Page	18, A Tribute to the Eighth Army (written in 1943)
Page	52, To Ann Harper in response to a letter from Australia
Page	52, To Grahame - welcome home from the Falklands
Page	85, Flo and Wal's Fortieth Wedding Anniversary
Page	92, Edie (1907 – 1970)

Politics

Page	20, The forgotten Dream

History, Nature and the Progress of the Human Race

Page	24, The Last Chance
Page	30, The adventures of a sine wave
Page	69, Nature
Page	77, Ode to the loss of Youthful Vigour

Seasonal Laments & Valentine's

Page	29, A Seasonal Lament
Page	32, Christmastide
Page	32, A Happy New Year

Page	65, Christmas and New Year – 1981
Page	66, The Music Center
Page	67, Easter Poems
Page	83, A Valentine Poem, Feb 14th 1996
Page	83, A Valentine Poem, Feb 14th 1997
Page	87, St. Valentine's Day 2000
Page	87, St. Valentine's Day 2001
Page	88, Another Valentine Poem
Page	88, Another Valentine Poem (2)
Page	62, Some more valentine poems
Page	101, St Valentine's day Feb 14th 2004
Page	49, Valentine Poems
Page	50, To my Valentine
Page	51, An early Valentine

Other poems, stuff and interesting bits!

Page	72, Anna
Page	88, A Limerick
Page	88, Oh, what a scandal

JUST A LITTLE FAMILY HISTORY

Sister Emily (no longer alive) was six years and six months old, Lilian was three years and one month and Ida was one year and three months old (more or less) the day I was born; a Saturday, the twenty seventh day of the month of June, 1907.

Emily died, stricken with cancer, at fifty three years of age. Lilian! now, or soon, to be seventy two, always, and still, the family rift—maker. Poor Ida, bereft of speech and only able to get out and about on a wheel chair.

Life plays grim tricks, but I presume, we all have our share of happiness, Ida now going through her grimmest time. I'm more contented than ever before. Lilian! I do not see, and so am not conversant with her but feel that she is morbid and unhappy, although she is rich in possessions. She constantly upsets Ida and caused friction between Crystal and her poor, helpless Mother.

Our Mother gave birth to two more children after my birth. When I reached the age of two years and three months, my brother Sidney was born. When he reached the age of four years, Gladys was born. She died whilst on holiday in Lisbon, killed by careless driving. The complete story remains a mystery. She was fifty three in the September of that year nineteen sixty seven. Gladys was my favorite and best loved sister and, with the years, I mourn her more. We two had decided to move to Saltdean but, on returning to London after a week end spent there, I heard of her tragic death. She left behind a husband, son and daughter, whom we now hardly ever see. Christmas and other holidays we often spent together, so, of-times, I felt I lost four people not just one.

Nineteen sixty seven had been a hard and difficult year. Alex and Sara closing down both factory and shop, almost bankrupt. He, terribly worried, and not knowing how we were going to manage. Eventually, we put our joint savings together, and bought this flat. It has turned out to be the most marvelous period in my life - getting to know neighborly people, leisure to read and write, to cook and enjoy the ordinary things of my life.

That old life never forgotten; the gay, the sad, the sordid, all that helped to make this person, the person I've turned out to be. Since the fifth of February, nineteen forty one, sharing my life with this Jewish man who formed the better me or rather, I should say, who also helped to form the woman I now am. Who proved so brave when his left arm was shattered by Hitler's bomb and I was blinded by blood and other injuries. But that bomb also now signifies true love that has lasted through the years .

That war, that year, nineteen forty one, March eighth, nine o 'clock at night, eating, drinking, laughing - the death of many but two lucky people who lived to tell the tale.

With the move to Saltdean and the death of a beloved sister; the gain of a brother. Parted for more than twenty years by that mischief, rift making sister. Despicable! I've renamed her. Sidney Connatty! looked up in the telephone book; a letter and he and his wife Violet came to see us. A very happy reunion it turned out to be. They live in Hove, only a short journey from Saltdean.

But now, more sadness to relate. Sid and Vi moved to Walmer, near Deal, Kent, to be near their son and his family. They loved their new home and Vi wrote many nice letters but, on the twenty fifth or twenty sixth of June, she died suddenly. I actually had a birthday card on the twenty seventh in her handwriting and posted on the twenty fifth or twenty sixth. Michael, their son, rang to tell me the tragic news. She was the nicest person I ever met in my life. Even 'Despicable' couldn't say anything unkind or untrue about her. When the row with Sid took place, Ida and her had tried to break up Sid and Vi's marriage.

Ida was very fond of Violet also and was always trying to let me know that she wanted Sid and Vi to visit her. Now, it is too late, but, if and when, Sidney visits us, I'll hope to bring Sister Ida and brother Sidney together at long last. It was 'Despicable's' quarrel not Ida's, but she took 'Despicable's' side.

MEMORIES OF SHANKLIN

Two cards from Shanklin, Isle of Wight,
Made me take up my pen to rhyme and write,
Nostalgic memories of Mother Dad, sisters Glad and Con,
Giving me plenty of thoughts to ponder on.

Dancing, moonlight bathing, loving the life I led,
Where are all those men? Perhaps dead.
John Beattie, Ernest Newton, A1 Milner, so many names,
Come to mind; John treated so badly to my everlasting shame.

That was life then — how much happier I am now,
With this dear man; gone are those eternal rows,
Lover's rows, family rows, plenty of grief,
Was it really me? It's beyond belief.

THE CONNATTYS

My Father's Father was Irish I'm convinced,
Left Ireland after the potato, famine feeling Che pinch.
He married and settled in Liverpool and many Connatty's were born,
Joseph Connatty went to London, sad and forlorn.
He met and married Emily Tisdall and six more Connatty's were born,
Not a very happy breed we turned out to be,
All determined to live our own lives and be free.
Life went by and what is past is past.
Sidney with his dear Violet,
Such a nice person, a real pet,
Ida lives quite near, strange they have not met,
Lilian lives in Worthing, a widow for many years,
Comfortably off and not many cares,
I live in Saltdean with Alex, visited by one or the other,
Ida is the one that causes most bother,
She has had a stroke and I try to be kind,
But there are times when she nearly drives me out of my mind.
Poor Crystal! What chance has she got?
Her Mother still tries to keep her brain washed.
My eldest sister Emily died from a cancer when she was fifty three.
Gladys died the same age when abroad with her family.
Three years have passed since this last sad event,
And in my heart it has made a large dent,
She was the sister I loved and cherished,
Even today I can hardly believe she has perished.
Written 7th October 1970

MEMORIES

In the Connatty family she was the fifth,
This child they named Edith,
At fifteen she was in love with love,
But the rain poured down from above.
Dave, the un—named, , Tony, came one after the other,
She simply had to be an unmarried Mother.
Her daughter she loved with all her heart,
From her she decided never to part.

Dave was her downfall, but now she is sure,

She was over—sexed and could never have been pure.
At twenty five she married very wrongly ,
As her love for Tony was going strongly ,
But now she does not regret the day,
He left her and went on his way..
No more sex she then resolved,
As her thoughts revolved and revolved,
The out of the blue that old friend turned up,
He took her for drinks and then to sup.
Hitler was out on the warpath that night,
Down came the bomb that put out the light,
Blood and slaughter brought heroes to the fore,
He earned her love that night and for evermore.
Since then, thirty years have gone ,
Still they are in love, still they have fun,
The light Hitler put out, he also put on.
When I look back at that old romance,
The memory pierces my heart like a lance,
The world was at war, nothing could last.
Yes! something did although his lot was cast,
When he walked out of my life that night,
Love and sex were finished, I was determined to fight.
But, soon everything was brighter,

In spite of Hitler's bombs and what we all went through,
Two old friends were re—united,
And our troth we gladly plighted.
For better or for worse it is often said.
For better it has been and happy are we,
At "Paradise Regained, Saltdean by the sea.

Written 19th or 20th July 1971

ODE TO AN ODE—MAKER
(From an admiring son—in—law)

She sits and writes poems and odes by the dozens,

Of grandchildren, sisters, aunts and her cousins,
Pontificates widely on seasons and weather,
Records for posterity her walks through the heather.

Nothing, it seems, can escape her attention,
She'll expound on any old subject you mention,
At the drop of a hat, she'll reach for her pen,
And she's off in a world of her Town once again.

Peopled with words, some good and some naughty,
Some sad and some happy, some friendly, some haughty,
She uses them all with considerable skill,
Bending and moulding them all to her will.

Yes, the odes of Nan Ramsey have earned wide acclaim,
If they've not brought her fortune, they've surely brought fame,
And her name will go down in the annals of time,
As a vastly prolific exponent of rhyme.

EDITH

I can see her standing in the hall,
Beautiful, elegant and tall,
She extended me a languid hand,
'Call me Edith,' -was her command.

The years have passed in slow procession,
Three grandchildren came in quick succession,
But, what with one thing and another,
It was always 'Edith,' never 'Mother'.

But, as her life force ebbed away,
And I held her hand that final day,
I felt at last, the time had come,
To squeeze that hand and call her 'Mum'.

(Both these poems read by Barrie at Edith's funeral 8/10/96)

In Loving Memory

THOUGHTS OF HOME

(Written in 1943 in a fit of nostalgia and patriotism)

Away from all the busy streets,
Along a mountain trail,
Through a pleasant, wooded glade,
Where the sun's rays often fail,
To penetrate the leafy roof,
That towers way up high,
A lonely meadow stands aloof,
Beneath an open sky,
'Tis there I find the real peace ,
That weary hearts oft yearn,
'Tis there all worldly worries cease,
'Tis there I would return.

Reposing there I'd be at ease ,
And command a widespread view,
Of vallies banked with leafy trees,
And streams of azure blue,
Of cottages where wreaths of smoke,
Rise up straight and high,
Rippled only now and then,
When a little breeze passed by.

As, in my mind, I see this scene,
The hand of nature wrought ,
The rolling hills, the pastures green,
I know now why they fought,
From covetous eyes and grasping hands,
They've fought for scenes like this,
They're fighting now in far off lands,
For the homes they love and miss,
And when they return from the sweat and toil,
They' have earned the right to say,
God put the British on this soil,
And here we'll damned well stay.
-July 9th 1943

BOYHOOD MEMORIES

How clearly I remember, the place where I was born,
The squeaky gate whereon I'd swing, the daisy strewn front lawn,
The homely aspidistra which was given pride of place,
In the front room by the window, draped and framed with lace.

Sixty four upon the door in highly polished brass,
Tubby, our old mongrel dog and romping in the grass,
The little family shop on the corner of the street,
Where I'd run my mother's errands for a ha'penny or a treat.

My uncle's photographic plates drying on the wall,
Our mobile grocer Tutton and his undeciphered call,
Grandma, stately as a queen, lovely, kind and sweet,
Grandpa, bowler hatted, mustachioed, small and neat.

Port Talbot nestles by the sea, cradled by a range of hills,
The summers of those childhood days were long and packed with thrills,
We'd swim and frolic in the waves and sunbathe on the sand,
Or tumble down the rolling dunes which lay twixt sea and land.

Or, maybe, when we'd tired of this, we'd turn to other pleasures,
And explore the inland mountains to search for hidden treasures,
Things like fossils, fairy dells or a long abandoned mine,
We'd penetrate the deep, dank depths and ignore the danger sign.

We built our dens high in the trees and played at Robin Hood,
We knew each secret hideaway and pathway through the wood,
Our hills were scarred with quarries for the stone that built our homes,
We'd scale their craggy heights and hack away at stones.

To watch them bounce and tumble 'till they hit the rock-strewn floor,
And, occasionally, we'd do the same and surface bruised and sore,
But ever we'd return again like moths drawn to a flame,
For thrills and spills were all a part of this our favorite game.

We made up games of make-believe and joined in heart and soul,
For reality was patched up clothes and workers on the dole,

Father, plodding through the streets, exposed to wind and rain,
His hopeless shrug which told us that his efforts were in vain.

No money there to pay the bills, mother pale and thin,
Whispers when the debtors call, 'Pretend there's no one in,
But she couldn't stop them taking her home for debts unpaid,
Mum and dad began to fight, their tempers short and frayed.

They parted, then returned again, but only for my sake,
Such is the toll of happiness society can take,
For, when poverty invades the home, love struggles to survive,
And only time and patience will keep the spark alive.

Yes, those were the days of the thirties, the days of deep depression,
Of, 'Buddy can you spare a dime?' and industrial recession
Of men sinking pride in their terrible need,
No task was too menial, nor desperate the deed.

But youth is immune to these down to earth shocks,
What if our toes poked clean through our socks ,
Our pants may be frayed, but we cared not a jot,
The world was our playground, the days long and hot.

Our local transport system was regarded with alarm,
They bounced and shook us mightily, but did us little harm,
They took us to the seaside, to Cwmavon through the hills,
To Neath and Pyle and Porthcawl for all the fairground thrills.

I remember too that one a week, the family'd gather around,
And in that family circle, true happiness was found,
While grandma played the piano and uncle Ray his cello,
Mum and dad would sing to us with voices sweet and mellow.

And then a good old sing—song which made the rafters part,
They made their own amusement - a long forgotten art,
The laughter and the talk were free from inhibition,
and the topics ranged from local chat to the U.S. prohibition.

I'd try my best to understand the things they talked of then,

But really it was most profound and quite beyond my ken,
The talk fades in the background to a soporific hum,
And the next thing I remember is , 'Come on. Wake up son.'

And when in bed I wait once more to board the Dream Man's train,
The sights and sounds of the day gone by, goes coursing through my brain,
The happy cries of children, the smell of fern and turf,
The golden sands, the azure sky, the thunder of the surf.

Happy childhood summer days, we thought not of the Winter,
We plucked the rose to breathe the scent and felt not thorn or splinter,
Would we could return once more to happy childhood joys,
And live again the carefree days we did when we were boys.

<u>A TRIBUTE TO THE R.A.F. (Written in 1943)</u>

A roar, a crash, a mighty sound,
Smote the still of the night,

It awakened the echoes far around,
And set the birds aflight.

For a moment I pondered on what it could be,
And then with growing pride,
I crossed to my window to see,
Them rise like a fast moving tide.

They were bombers spreading avenging wings,
Vultures after prey,
Black, powerful monstrous things ,
That seemed inclined to play,
As they dodged in and out of the windswept clouds,
But seldom went astray.

Oh, how I thrilled as I watched that sight,
And remembered just two years ago,
Almost the only planes in flight,
Were the bombers of the foe.

And how, as weeks and months went by,
Our power steadily grew,
'Till we become the masters Of the sky,
We, who once were the few.

And now the tables turn,
Cities that once grew vain,
Crumble, totter, fall and burn,
And cry aloud in pain.

And our planes shall darken every door,
That hides a Fascist there,
And bombs shall fall still more and more,
As more planes take the air.

And as I crept back to my bed,
I raised a little prayer,
For those brave men who tinge skies red,
With the fire they start down there.

For I recall what the Premier said,
And realized he knew,
That someday, though we sweat and bled,
A host would replace the few.

A TRIBUTE TO THE EIGHTH ARMY (written in 1943)

Through miles of stony, sand—swept tracks,
In grit and grime they fight,
With heavy packs upon their backs,
They trek through day and night,
Relentlessly pursuing a treacherous foe,
Who knows no code or rule,
Harassing him wherever he goes,
Stubborn as a mule.

Bombarding him with heavy guns,
And giving him no rest,
Two thousand miles advanced the 'Eighth',
Then came their greatest test.

At the Mereth Line the armies met,
And parried blow for blow,
It is a fight we shan't forget,
The fierceness of it so.

How gallantly that army fought,
Who just three years ago,
Were citizens who never thought,
Of fighting such a foe.

But the enemy was beaten back,
And the 'Eighth' resumed advance.

Hitting the Germans, who in the past,
Had led them such a dance.

And, here in Britain, every night,
A little prayer we raise,

In Loving Memory

To those brave men who won this fight,
And ask of us no praise.

"Oh God, that day when thou decree,
This fateful war shall end,
And when the world is once more free,
And broken hearts will mend.

Restore the 'Eighth' to the ones they love,
And we'll cherish the memory,
Of the gallant way that these men fought,
To keep our country free.

TO MY DARLING WIFE IN EVERLASTING APPRECIATION AND GRATITUDE FOR GIVING ME SUCH A LOVELY SON, DAVID.

I lay in silence in the night,
Until the first, gray streaks of light,
Filtered through the window pane,
Another day was here again.

The sun, a glowing fireball rose,
Above yon hill in stately pose,
And settled down to ride on high,
Its eternal journey through the sky.

This day - no different from the rest,
And yet beloved - for ever blessed,
Remembered ever, come what may,
Because our son was born this day.

The tenth of the second 'forty nine',
Zero five zero was the time,
And on this youthful Thursday morn,
A lovely baby boy was born.

I learned this all a few hours later,
And never has my joy been greater,

I was like a king upon a throne,
This day was ours and ours alone.

Then a calm descended on me there,
And I offered up a little prayer,
Thanking God for bringing you,
Unharmed, unchanged and safely through.

And David, angelic, lovely child,
Like God's own Son both meek and mild,
We'll love him through the passing years,
Sharing all his joy and tears.

Our prayers were answered, so it seems,
Beyond our maddest, wildest dreams,
I'm a Daddy, you're a Mummy,
It's hard to believe, it still feels funny.

But the greatest thrills are yet in store,
When first he crawl upon the floor,
And one day he'll say 'Mum' or 'Dad',
If 'Mum' comes first, I'll get so mad.

And now my darling, here's a toast,
I'll drink throughout my life,
'Here's to the ones I love the most,
My son, my lovely wife'.

THE FORGOTTEN DREAM

Hey you, yes you on strike,
Let me tell you what it was like,
When workers slaved from dusk til dawn,
In the days long ago, before you were born.

You have never suffered the degradation,
Of having to keep to one's own station,
Touching the forelock to the local squire,
For he had the power to hire or fire.

They coughed up their lungs in dust laden mines,
Up dark, sooty chimneys the small boy climbs,
Hungry and shivering, the menial clerk,
Trudges home in the gathering dark.

Thin, ragged kids at mansion gates ,
Hungrily gaze on the food-laden plates,
And fight like wild wolves over scraps at them hurled,
By people who live in a different world.

Finally, driven to distraction,
Some decide on industrial action,
And finished counting up the cost,
In casualties of a battle lost.

The bosses knew they had them beaten,
Knew that when they hadn't eaten,
They'd come crawling back upon their knees,
And beg for their jobs with piteous pleas.

You couldn't beat the system with isolated action,
They had to act in unity, not as a tiny faction,
So 'Workers of the world, unite',
Became the slogan of the coming fight.

For organized they had the strength,
To carry the fight to any length,
And the bosses had to face this fact,
When they asked the strikers for a pact.

Joyous were the celebrations,
Forgotten the trials and tribulations,
The meek, subjective days were past,
They had the power to fight at last.

But all was not a bed of roses,
On both sides there were bloodied noses ,
But conditions improved and the workers life,
No longer consisted of torment and strife.

The unions went from strength to strength,
Years past, until at length,
Into politics they went,
And formed a new party in parliament.

Then began the legislation,
To make this land a socialist nation,
The high ideals of the past were dead,
Spite and dogma ruled instead.

Then the Marxists, Trots and Lefties,
And a potpourri of aggressive hefties,
Spotted their chance to run the nation,
Through a process of infiltration.

How they must have laughed with joy,
At the weakness which allowed this ploy,
The complacency which, in the end, had led,
To a bunch of Reds in the Labour bed.

In Loving Memory

So, you on strike, you poor fool,
Don't you know you're just a tool,
An implement in the endless quest,
To raise the red flag in the west.

Ambulance men, where is your code?
Can you leave the injured on the road,
To bleed until their lives are spent,
For an extra three or four percent?

You miners. What's your excuse today,
In striking for that extra pay?
Can you stand by and watch the old,
Shivering and dying in the cold.

You power workers - you demand your rights,
By putting out the country's lights,
Boasting in frustrated rage,
You'd take us back to the dark stone age.

And civil servants with the best intentions,
Withhold the public service pensions,
And water workers threaten us,
With divers plagues disastrous.

They're all there, hammering at the door,
Greedy palms stretched out for more ,
Manipulated puppets on a string,
Jumping to do the union thing.

You on strike, you know at heart,
Your actions are tearing this country apart,
With your fingers closed around her throat,
Remember, we're all in the self - same boat.

Only you, the working man ,
Can frustrate their malevolent plan,
Show you're made of stronger stuff,
Stand up to them and cry, 'Enough!

We want to work and earn our pay,
Not face disruption every day,
So workers of the world, unite,
And stop this suicidal fight.

THE LAST CHANCE

Return with me to yesteryear,
When travelers ventured forth in fear,
For danger and discomfort lay,
In store for them on the king's highway.

In stages rattling through the dark,
In rutted tracks, o'er moorland stark,
Robbed and plundered on the way,
By felons on the king's highway.

It was, indeed, no time to roam,
And, mostly, people stayed at home,
But sometimes circumstances bade,
That journeys such as this be made.

My tale concerns a battered stage,
Whose passengers, consumed with rage,
Had suffered all this privatization,
And longed to reach the coaching station.

And when, at last, they saw grow near,
The mellow lights of warmth and cheer,
It was, indeed, a blessed sight,
A haven in the storm of night.

Then, when their appetites were sated,
The talk was loud and animated,
They drank the landlord's finest ale,
And each one told a sorry tale.

A tale of dangers men must face,
When traveling from place to place,
And each one prayed the day would dawn,
When speed and comfort were the norm.

And then a voice spoke from the gloom,
Of the furthest corner of the room,
'Good travelers, be content this day,
For you know not, that for which you pray'.

And, peering into the gloom, they spied,
A man of dignity and pride,
Who rose and came toward them now,
Giving each a courtly bow.

'Your pardon, sirs, if I intrude,
I pray you will not think me rude,
I've journeyed far to reach this day,
So bear with me, good friends, I pray.

'I tell you now 'tis in my power,
To grant your wish this very hour,
But if I do, I make it clear,
You'll lose the things you hold most dear.

The air you breathe is clean and sweet,
The countryside unspoiled and neat,
Your children play away from danger ,
And folk show kindness to a stranger.

The oak, the elm and ash abound,
In forest glade wild life is found,
The rivers stocked with fish run clear,
All things proclaim that God is near.

I've listened to your tales of woe,
And tell you now, all this will go,
For, in pursuance of his greed,
Man goes beyond his basic need.

So hark, good folk, while I relate,
The future that will be your fate,
For I have seen such things take place,
And the degradation of the human race.

It all begins when man's great dream,
Takes shape with engines run by steam,
And harnessing this latent power,
They traveled many miles an hour.

Puffing through the pastures green,
They presented quite a pleasant scene,
While in their wake they pulled along,
A happy and contented throng.

At last the travelers were secure,
Their journey's end was safe and sure,
Smoothly , comfortably they rode,
And forgot the perils of the road.

But this was not enough it seems,
Speed was the essence of all schemes ,
Men strove to find the quickest way,
To travel on the queen' s highway.

And so we reach another age .
The horseless carriage is the rage,
Now, frantically, both rail and road,
Compete for passengers and their load.

And like some monstrous thing unchained,
Road and rail ran unrestrained,
Linking towns from coast to coast,
'Expansion, Progress' is the boast.

Now the populace explodes,
The peaceful way of life erodes,
And powerless to stop the boom,
The world is hastened to its doom.

People through the air were hurled,
On metal wings that spanned the world,
The roads became more saturated,
And pollution spread out unabated.

Cars belched fumes and chimneys smoked,
Folks no longed laughed and joked,
There was anger, terror in their faces,
They yearned for peace and quiet places.

Their foolish use of God-sent gifts,
Had led to international rifts,
Life was held in low esteem,
And peace was but an empty dream.

They reached out for the very stars,
And spaceships scanned the planet Mars,
While life on Earth grew more uncertain,
And divided by an 'iron curtain'.

Now people wait with bated breath,
For the power over life and death,
Is in the hands of every nation,
To use for good or desolation.

So now, my friends, choose well this day,
Have those things for which you pray,
But heed, I beg, my sound advice,
Or be prepared to pay the price.

The clock ticked loud upon the wall,
And flickering shadows touched them all,
Immobilized as in a trance ,
They gazed upon the man askance.

Then, suddenly, the spell was broken,
They blinked like men but lately woken,
The cameo sprang to life anew,
And the hum of conversation grew.

'How know you this,' exclaimed mine host,
Art thou wizard or a ghost?'
'Neither, friend,' the stranger said,
'Do I look like one quite dead?

But, neither am I one of thee,
I'm from the time to come, you see,
And so I know what lies in store,
If you choose the path to strife and war.

Raucous laughter filled the air,
'Ye gods,' cried one, 'he's not all there,
Does he take us all for frails,
To listen to his prattling tales.

'Be gone old man, or hold thy peace,
And let this fortune telling cease,'
So saying this, they turned away,
To drink and laugh the night away.

But day must dawn, and once again,
They're on their way through wind and rain,
Praying that they soon will see,
An end to all this misery.

Breathing deep of the clean, fresh air ,
The stranger heard their fervent prayer ,
He knew now that he'd lost his case,
And hope had died for the human race.

'If only man would realise,
To just stand still is sometimes wise,
He shrugged and gave a heartfelt sigh,
'There was just a chance' I had to try.

And then a low, pulsating sound,
Pervaded all the air around,
And locals, faces white with fear,
Watched the stranger disappear.

A SEASONAL LAMENT (written in 1978)

Where are the springs that once we knew?
When the days grew warm and the skies turned blue,
And the last snows melting on the hill,
Fed each swollen stream and rill.

When the morning chorus shrilled at five,
And bees prepared to leave the hive,
And flowers wakening one by one,
Turn to face to rising sun.

Then will we, once again, behold,
Cherry pink and laburnum gold,
Blossoms of each shade and hue,
Outlined against a sky of blue.

But now those skies stay cold and gray ,
And the wind blows from the north each day,
If the sun shines, it's a nine day's wonder,
To be followed by a week of thunder.

Tulips and daffodils bent in pain,
Lashed by constant wind and rain,
The fields are squelching seas of mud,
And rivers burst their banks in flood.

Each year we hope for better things,
For earlier and warmer springs,
And while we shiver with the cold,
We dream again of the springs of old.

Days of sunshine, buds and flowers,
Daisy chains and happy hours,
And I wonder if they'll come again,
As I gaze though my rain lashed window pane.

THE ADVENTURES OF A SINE WAVE

My story is a sad one. Hark to my tale of woe,
Of how a shapely Sine Wave degenerated so.
It happened in an instant, but in that time my friends ,
They took my form and used it to achieve their devious ends.

When the summons came I answered, as all good Sine Waves do,
I started out along my route, which was Via PL2.
Emerging from pin twenty four, happily I sped,
When, suddenly a traffic jam I spied just up ahead.

I put on all the anchors, but ever on-wards ploughed,
And at a steady rate of knots, I plunged into the crowd.
Pushed and shoved and jostled, I was swallowed in the fray,
Then, ruffled and bedraggled, I was once more on my way.

Slightly dazed and shaken, I rushed to make up time,
Then, suddenly I noticed, a grid upon the line.
It blocked my way, I could not pass, and other Sine Waves too,
Crowded up behind me, and began to form a queue.

Soon I felt my lovely shape, collapse and lose its form,
As electron by electron, through this object I was drawn.
My road was gone - I found myself in an airless void enclosed,
Caught up and hurled with other shapes, similarly disposed.
My particles were scattered, my heart was filled with dread,
Remorselessly we were propelled to whatever lay ahead.
And then a strange thing happened, I seemed to grow and grow,
Built up and expanded by the electrons in the flow.

Then suddenly, the rush was gone, silence reigned supreme,
I viewed, once more before me, the old familiar scene.
Just up ahead, another jam was forming on the road,
But this time I was ready, and passed safely through the load.

These hazards all behind me, I sped serenely on,
And then it was I released my previous shape was gone.
I had become enormous, and carved in half at that,
Gone were all my graceful curves and what was left was flat.

'What have they done to me,' I cried. 'They've hurt me to the core,
From a thing of passing beauty, I'm a square pulse, nothing more.'
With heavy heart I carried on, and spied ahead a gate,
Where other pulses just like me, were rushing in a spate.

I was caught up in the torrent, and joined the mad rat-race,
But just as I approached the gate, it slammed shut in my face.
'Well, here's a fine to do, I thought. 'How do I get through that?'
When the gate was opened once again, and through it I was spat.

Immediately I was pounced upon, and in that awesome fray,
A hundred nasty, spiky things joined me on the way.
I had now become a clock pulse, a hundred hertz or so,
'To think,' I thought' 'that in this form, through my whole life I must go.

But fate had other plans for me, and pulled out every stopper,
As if they hadn't done enough, they passed me through a chopper.
They cut me into little bits and sent me on my way,
On the last lap of my Journey; this was to be my day.

For this great moment I was born, and it gave me quite a kick,
As I sped into that solenoid, and made the counter click.
But, oh the cost, the grief, the woe to perform that simple task,
But just to do it once again, is all that I could ask.

CHRISTMASTIDE

Oh Vicki, dear Vicki, the season's here again,
Of Christmas trees and fairy lights and frosty window panes,
Of happy folks and family jokes and parties at the hearth,
Of children singing carols and snow upon the path.

The holly and the mistletoe, the tinsel and the braid,
On specially cleared mantelshelves, the Christmas cards arrayed,
The bar's well stocked, the larder's full, the goodies all on view,
A season of togetherness with friends both old and new.

Happy, joyful Christmastide, how eagerly we wait,
The atmosphere of peace and love your season will create,
And so this message comes to you, time honored and sincere,
A very merry Christmas and a prosperous new year.

A HAPPY NEW YEAR! (24/1/78)

On new year's eve at the appropriate time,
We all clasped hands — sang Auld Lang Syne,
Then raised our drinks and gave a cheer,
And welcomed in the brave new year.

Since then it's been a tale of woe,
We lost the dog - she had to go,
Then came the first of ills to blight us,
And Dad went down with acute bronchitis.

In Loving Memory

As a result of this, poor Dave and Jill,
Themselves became a trifle ill,
They sniffed a gave explosive sneezes,
And, occasionally, asthmatic wheezes.

Then, as if this wasn't quite enough,
Mum, who's made of sterner stuff,
Scorning colds - got out of bed,
And promptly slipped a disc instead.

So, I swear, the next one that I meet,
Who wishes me with smile so sweet,
'A happy and a bright new year,'
I'll punch him 'round the flipping ear!'

MY BEST FRIENDS.
(Written by Joan Caruana)

Sitting in the Astra one cold November night,
A lady did but speak to us, which started us off right,
A friend in the making she turned out to be,
When, next day, she came for a cup of coffee.

The albums came out, and it does seem,
She had a son where my husband had been,
She then produced pictures 1,2,3 of the finest sons one ever did see,
Then came Dad, lean as could be, to add to the tales of sons 1,2 and 3.

To Berlin we went and Wick did come,
Bearing with her No. 3 son,
To Brandenberg Gate we did go,
Dragging Grahame along in tow.

'It won't be far,' Aunty said,
And old Grahame did drop his head.
Gate we reach with much ado,
Charlie wants to go to loo.

Later we do meet,
In house we bought just up the street,
Cookies move in Beaumont Drive,
Gee, it's great to be alive.

Christmas, New Year too,
We met and laughed as many do,
'Till Malta bound we went one day,
High in the sky and far away.

Wick, Barrie, Mum, Alex too,
There is none we miss as much as you,
Friends have come and friends have gone,
But Wick and Barrie still go on.

ABSENT FRIENDS

Dear Charles and dear Joan,
Why did you leave us all alone?
Why did you take a plane and soar,
Away to Malta's sunny shore?

We miss your happy, smiling faces,
We miss you in the strangest places,
We miss you when we pass your door,
In Marks and Spencer's high - class store.

I miss Joan's blonde, curly thatch,
Vicki misses Charles' bald patch,
We both miss the comfort and content,

That having friends close by once meant.

Your faces stare at us from snaps,
A little younger then perhaps,
Evoking memories sweet and pleasant,
From '54 up to the present

Once more we're back in dear old Celle,
When Grahame was just a little fella,
And oh, the sweet, nostalgic pain,
To live that Christmas once again.

And all the other pictures too,
Of Christmases we've spent with you,
Showing food and drink galore,
Makes us miss you all the more.

So book that trip and take that plane,
And visit your old pals again,
And leave us just a little more,
To add to friendship's memory store.

WHEN JACKIE MARRID GRAHAME (1973)

Grahame's getting married,
Goodness, what a shock,
parents looking harried,
He's doing it on the Rock.

That Mum and I must go.
There can be little doubt,
Now the bank account is very low,
But, at least, we're going out.

Set off like a king and queen,
In a mood of quiet euphoria,
At Gravesend, caught the twelve eighteen,
To get us to Victoria.

At Charring Cross came the drops of rain,
That herald the gathering storm,
With Mum aboard, out pulls the train,
And left me stranded on the platform.

Now Vicki's lost her ticket,
She's lost her hubby too,
She's on a sticky wicket,
And doesn't know what to do.

So, true to form, at times like these,
When things look bleak and hope just dies out,
What does Mum do, if you please?
She sits her down and cries her eyes out.

So, thus I find her on the station,
Filling buckets with her tears,
I whisper words of consolation,
And endeavor to allay her fears.

So the situation is righted,
And on our way we're heading,
To board a plane at Gatwick sited,
Which will fly us to our Grahame's wedding

Howrah! Gibraltar here we come,
The plane is fling straight and high,
The engine's tone a drowsy hum,
Look, Madrid's just passed us by.

Then came the captain's voice so glib,
Urging us to have no fear,
But, as we couldn't land at Gib.,
He'd have to divert to Tangier.

Below, the sea's a wonderous sight,
Spume spraying from the frothing foam,
Captives flying through the night,
Feeling lost and far from home.

In Loving Memory

Bumping, lurching through the sky,
The plane heads for the distant shore,
We're there - The runway flashes by,
The brakes applied, the engines roar.

So, here we are, all milling 'round,
The airport lounge in old Tangier,
It wasn't long before I found,
It cost twelve shillings for a beer.

At the hotel Minzah where we stayed,
Room number one—oh—two,
The time passed slowly, I'm afraid,
There was little we could do.

Our temporary taste of Tangier's joys,
Might have proved unbeatable,
But for the noise of the market boys,
And the food, which was uneatable.

On Wednesday morning rumors bounced,
Like echoes in a mountain chain,
And then a Rep. at last announced,
'Passengers, you're on your way again.

'This time you'll have to go by sea,
The wind is still quite high,
I said, 'We'll be in Gib. by tea,'
And Mother had a quiet cry.

At half past one the Mons Calpe sails,
Mum is drinking to forget,
There are passengers wailing at the rails,
And we haven't left the harbor yet.

But soon our journey's end's in sight,
I keep my fingers crossed,
Hoping Grahame's there alright,
To meet us, or we're lost.

But there he is, our son so dutiful,
A welcome sight to see,
And with him, looking very beautiful,
His lovely bride to be.

poor Grahame, wondering when his folks would land,
Meeting every plane and ship,
Spoiling all the things he'd planned,
A Roy Hudd show, a tourist trip.

But now the waiting time is done,
And oh, it's good to see once more,
Our sturdy, suntanned, smiling son,
And to meet our future daughter-in-law.

And what a pleasure too to see,
Jackie's Mum and Dad,
We took to them immediately,
And think our son's a lucky lad.

At the youngster's 'penthouse' where we stayed,
We viewed their starting things with pleasure,
The #fridge stocked up, the pans arrayed,
The toiletries, the things they treasure.

Now by this time we nursed a yen,
The local hooch to savor,
So they took us to a little den,
With a marked judicial flavour.

A noose or two was hanging around,
Legal beagles from the walls did peer,
Courtly robes and scrolls abound,
And folks passed judgment on the beer.

And so to bed in sweet content,
Asleep in Morpheus' soft caress,
Suddenly the night's still air is rent,
By the howls of a babe in dire distress.

In Loving Memory

Poor kids, think I, if they hear this,
It's an even bet that maybe,
'Twill shatter their dreams of conjugal bliss,
And they'll never have a baby.

Tonight our Grahame spreads his wings,
And has a booze - up with the boys,
We threaten him with dire things,
If he comes home drunk or makes a noise.

So parents, not to be outdone,
Have a booze - up of their own,
At the 'Huntsman' recommended by our son,
Who seems to know each bar in town.

But he later gives us quite a shock,
For, far from raising up a riot,
Bless his little cotton sock,
He was sober and extremely quiet.

And so we come to the wedding eve,
Jack comes home tired and harried,
Time to relax; it's hard to believe,
Tomorrow they'll be married.

So, consoled by the thought that we'd not lost a son,'
But gained a most beautiful daughter,
The parents drift to the mess for some fun,
While the kids stay at home in quarter.

As ex R.A.F. it was good once again,
To have a night out in the mess,
It's a feeling that's quite hard to explain,
You could call it nostalgia I guess.

Instantly we felt at home,
And the drinks flowed thick and fast,
I even met a chap I'd known,
In the not-so-distant past.

So, happy in our little heaven,
Time passed us by on wings of light,
But we'd agreed we must go at eleven,
'Twould never do to retire tight.

Now presently our Mum's dear face,
Took on a greeny hue,
Her eyes went glazed, and just in case,
She was shown the way to the ladies loo.

Then promptly at the appointed time,
I phoned for the local hack,
But when it came our Mum said, 'I'm,
Staying the night with Maud and Jack.

And now we come to the bitter bit,
Should I go or should I stay?
I went and felt an awful twit,
Going off alone that way.

'But then, I do remember thinking,
Vicki will be going too,
Little did I know the drinking,
Would continue until way past two.

In Loving Memory

So here we have the classic tale,
Of Mums, who in a trice,
Warn their kids, then blithely fail,
To heed their own advice.

And when the gray, cold night is spent,
Feeling low and far from hearty,
She's wondering where the gay girl went,
Who sparkled brightly at the party.
At the guardroom where they'd normally hurl,
Drunken folks inside,
The staff were good to our wayward girl,
And a taxi for her hied.

But then, before the car arrived,
An officer drew near,
He said, 'My dear, I've just derived,
In need of help you are I hear.

I'm going to town, so hop in do,
And off he sped with the parent,
Passing the taxi driver who,
Would be wondering where his fare went.

so soon our Mum stood there before us,
As cheerful as could be,
'Welcome home,' we cried in chorus,
'Come and have a cup of tea'

And so we come to the wedding day,
In humour it's begun,
I pray it carries on that way,
Today and all the days to come.

While son takes Dad for a trip up the Rock,
Mum's off to do some shopping,
We stop at the top, while I take stock,
Of the View Which is simply 'topping'.

But the sands of time are running out,
On Grahame's Bachelor days,
That all things change, there is no doubt,
He's at the parting of the ways.

At the church the scene is set,
A little knot of folk outside,
Include the passengers we met,
All waiting there to see the bride.

Inside the congregation waits,
And organ music fills the air,
The vicar hopes the bride's not late,
While the bridegroom breathes a silent prayer.

Then suddenly the music swells,
The Wedding March booms forth with pride,
The joyous clamour of the bells,
Heralds the arrival of the bride.

And here she come with radiant face,
As one the congregation stands ,
Jack leaves the aisle to take his place,
And bride and groom stand touching hands.

I've yet to see a bride so fair,
Or a groom so proud and straight,
A handsome couple standing there,
Waiting to fulfill their fate .

Down Mum's face the tears just poured,
And, glancing at her pew,
I thankfully observed that Maud,
Was quietly weeping too.

So Jacqueline Rosemary Helen,
Married Grahame Barrie Cooke,
And soon we all got 'fell in'
To sign the registrar book.

In Loving Memory

The book was signed, the deed was done,
We wished them joy and sweet content,
Jackie and Grahame were truly one,
And the cameras clicked to record the event.

The confetti rained from left and right,
And a wag cried from afar,
' I know what Cookie's doing tonight,
He's cleaning out the CO's car.

And now, to express our appreciation,
To Jack for arranging the reception,
The cake and food were a revelation,
Which all enjoyed without exception.

We wined and dined, and I thought with pride,
Of our lucky Grahame who,
Not only got a lovely bride,
But darned good in-laws too.

The cake was cut, the toasts went down,
And we all arranged to meet,
Later at a club in town,
The locals called 'The Fleet'.

If I known what the place was like,
I'd have made a good excuse,
For being somewhere in the Klondike,
Or becoming a confirmed recluse.

'Cos boy! the noise that came from there,
Howls and shrieks like dogs with rabies,
Split and rent the tortured air,
And Mum retired to the 'ladies'.

We stuck it for about an hour,
For the sake of the couple newly wed,
Hoping the amplifier's power,
Would fail, or the singer, maybe, drop down dead.

But the pace continued hot as hades,
So, dreaming of a peaceful brew,
We went and fetched Mum from the ladies',
And to the Sergeant's Mess withdrew.

The masochistic ways of youth,
I'll never get their measure,
They go through hell and then, forsooth,
They even pay for the dubious pleasure.

In the mess we settled down in style,
To have a peaceful sup,
We laughed and chatted for a while,
And then the party livened up.

Someone there of tact bereft,
Remembered Jack had sworn,
A fearful oath, that ere he left,
The 'Stripper' he'd perform.

And so the trickster crept away,
To sort the record out,
And when the tune began to play,
Jack blanched and sought the best way out.

But he released there was no escape,
And, though Maud was in a rage,
He proceeded there and then to ape,
The strippers of the stage.

His torso waved in slow procession,
And he started to remove,
His shoes and socks in quick succession,
He was really in the groove.

His jacket, shirt and tie came next,
As he whirled around thew floor,
Maud was looking very vexed,
While the audience yelled for more.

He doffed his vest, the music swelled,
And he didn't turn a hair,
When Maud, as pink as sunset yelled,
'Jack Hutton, don't you dare!'

Down zipped his flies and therein peeked,
Striped pants of many hues,
The females in the audience shrieked,
For more expansive views.

Maud was busy throwing things,
And I quietly withdrew,
My beer from her range of swings,
Or she'd have hurled that too.

So Jack thought he'd best refrain,
Ere Maud improved her shot,
So, zipping up his pants again,
He cried, 'Folks, that your lot.'

Then Jack turned round to find his gear,
He'd removed with much aplomb,
Was being worn by something queer,
Which soon turned out to be our Mum.

And so this day draws to its close,
A truly happy day,
Content we nestle in repose,
And quietly dream the night away.

Next day we wandered down to see,
The brand new married pair,
At hte Caleta Palace by the sea,
In temporary residence there.

On the way back to the quarter,
The concrete catchments stood resplendent,
Smooth surfaces to catch the water,
To make Gibraltar independent.

Then Grahame filled us with dismay,
By announcing there and then,
A game of rugby he would play,
While Jackie washed her hair.

We thought, 'Good lord, He's flipped his lid,'
He's never got the strength,
But he vowed he'd play, and play he did,
And even scored a try at length.

On a concrete pitch they had to play,
And the game was fast and gory,
The away team won the day,
But Grahame captured all the glory.

That night we danced with the happy two,
At their hotel by the sea,
Both Mum and I were happy too,
And proud as anyone could be.

In happiness, time flies they say,
We've Just a few hours more,
So much to see in one short day,
So many areas to explore.

St. Michael's cave, the Barbary apes,
The galleries and the Moorish tower,
The Spanish and Moroccan capes,
The relics of Britannia's power.

We saw them all in a breathless whirl,
And marveled at the sights,
We watched the British flag unfurl,
And proudly fly on rocky heights.

Now time has gone, the knell has tolled,
We're at the airport with our new - found friends,
Just one drink ere we leave the fold,
And our happy, carefree sojourn ends.

In Loving Memory

Just then the Tannoy's strident call,
Informed us, as the time was near,
To get ourselves along the hall,
To show the customs we were clear.

Then the gates clanged shut behind us,
And we were subjected to a search,
Now, in the airport lounge you'll find us,
Left completely in the lurch.

We could only wave a last farewell,
Behind a door of glass,
Confined within our airport cell,
Things had reached a pretty pass.

Dusk has settled o'er the land,
Goodbye Cookies, Maud and Jack,
The holiday's been really grand,
Maybe next year we'll be back.

And so we're airborne once again,
The Rock dips over the horizon,
Heading homewards over Spain,
The Trident quickly, smoothly flies on.

So, here we are all milling 'round,
The airport lounge in London town,
It wasn't long before we found,
A strike had slowed the baggage down.

I didn't own our Mum that night,
She'd donned a fez to have some fun,
Jill said to Dave, 'I think she's tight,
I'd shoot her if I had a gun.

A full two hours we had to wait,
Before our luggage came,
While all the time I cursed my fate,
And swore I'd never fly again.

so now at two am you'll find us,
Speeding swiftly out of town,
But we hadn't left our cares behind us,
For now the car has broken down.

We confined the thing to all hell's fires,
The language used was coarse and rife,
We pulled some wires and kicked the tyres,
And then the engine sprang to life.

And so we went the last few miles,
In a sweat of apprehension,
But now we're home, we're full of smiles,
The rest's not worth a mention.

Except to say my tale is done,
With its blend of joy and mayhem,
We'll not forget those days of fun,
When Jackie married Grahame.

ADDENDUM TO THE ABOVE

There was a young airman named Grahame,
Whose technique with girls would just slay 'em,
But he went to Gibraltar,
Got led to the altar,
And if he knows any prayers he 'd best pray 'em.

A FORLORN HOPE

Don't emulate the rabbit,
And make this thing a habit,
But, if you really think you aughter,
Please make just one a daughter.

VALENTINE POEMS

I only have one Valentine,
And, darling, that is you,
My love, my heart, my all is thine,
And it comes from - shhh - you know who.

Flowers to brighten up the hours,
And help to drive the blues away,
Beauty to dissipate the showers,
And cheer you gently on your way.
14th August 1986

(To be sung to the tune of 'Be my baby bumble bee)

Be my baby Valentine,
I love you, you love me - least, I hope you do,
I will love you all the time,
Yes I will, yes I will; yes I always will,

I would like to spend my days,
praising all your loving ways ,
Then if you should love me back, I'd thrill,
Yes I will, yes I will; yes indeed I will.

You have always been the one ,
Only you, only you; no one else but you,
And when all is said and done,
I want you, I want you; no one else will do.

Set my loving heart aglow,
Tell me I'm your only beau,
And I'll love you my baby valentine.
14th February 1984

The moon and stars I promised you,
I promised you the skies,
And now I know it's all come true,
For I see them in your eyes.

TO MY VALENTINE
(From Vicki to me – 13/02/46)

There are no words lovely enough,
Or rich enough ; there is no way,
For me to clothe in language, love,

All the things my heart would say.

And so I send a card that wears,
Red ribbons and a flippant heart,
An airy bit of lace around,
Saucy Cupid and his dart.

And there's a bit of verse that reads:
'Won't you be my Valentine,'
But the sweet, the true, the tender words,
Read them, love, between each line.

AN EARLY VALENTINE
(Date unknown)

You may seek him far,
Or seek him near,
The one who sends this card from here,
But, look around, he's close to you,
Always loving, always true.

MOTHER'S DAY

I realise that being a Dad,
Excuses me from dates like this,
But I somehow feel the kids we've had,
Are bound to give this day a miss.

So it falls upon long suffering me,
To shoulder these affairs of state,
And represent those forgetful three,
On this most auspicious Mother's date.

Just a little verse to say.
A happy Mother's day,
A thought for all the love you've shared,
The many ways you shown you cared.

A Mother's love and deep devotion,

Is an emotion strong as any potion,
And so for just this short, sweet day,
We remember - but we can't repay.

TO ANN HARPER IN RESPONSE TO A LETTER FROM AUSTRALIA

To help this land in times of doubt,
We sacrificed a lot,
We been told to: 'Get that light out!'
And till our little plot.

We've been told to - Be like Dad; keep Mum,
Exhorted to economize,
Told we're better off than some,
When we know it's all a pack of lies.

'Switch off something now,' they say,
'To save a little light,
Gone is Britain's heyday,
We pull our belts up tight.

As a nation we're a failure,
And things have reached a pretty pass,
When told by people in Australia,
To wipe our bums with tufts of grass.

TO GRAHAME - WELCOME HOME FROM THE FALKLANDS

Welcome home son, missed you so,
Out there in all that ice and snow,
Struggling in a force eight storm,
While we were tucked up snug and warm.

Thought of in the Atlantic swell,
Trust you kept your food down well,
Living in a tent on compo rations,
Enough to douse the strongest passions.

In Loving Memory

Sorry your aerials blew down son,
But, as the actress said after a little fun,
'Bishop, you've had your wicked ways,
But I've managed to hang on to my stays.'

And now you 're back in your family fold,
Soon to be off again I'm told,
Gibraltar may be many miles,
But it's not as cold as the Falkland Isles.

WHEN DAVID PLAYED FOR ENGLAND AGAINST WALES

'What went wrong?' I ask myself,
He had the best upbringing,
I'm limp - feel left upon the shelf,
When I should be really singing.

And what's upset all that I'd planned?
What's brought about my wails?
My son's just played for England,
Against my homeland Wales.

Thus I have my just rewards,
I'm punished for my sins,
To cheer on Gareth Edwards,
And hope that England wins.

(What a dilemma) 1976

LAURA

Dearest, sweetest baby Laura,
How could one help but to adore her,
Doll-like, delicate as china,
Was there ever baby finer?

Skin as soft as thistledown,
Brow creased in a little frown,
How big, how strange this wonderous world,
Into which you've just been hurled.

Little finger curled round mine,
Fills me with a love sublime,
And when she's cradled in my arms,
I •m captive of her winsome charms.

Dearest Laura, new arrival,
Your beauty will be hard to rival,
At birth you tore a spell apart,
And weaved another 'round my heart.

In Loving Memory

ODES TO MUM WHEN SHE'S AWAY.
'TILL THEN.

'Till then, 'Till you return home once more,
'Till then, dust will pile on the floor,
'Till then, I'll sit and just raise a snore,
'Till you return.

'Till then, no more will I sit and freeze,
'Till then, no scrubbing floors on my knees,
'Till then, I'll do once more as I please,
'Till you return.

Although there are dishes I must soak,
And windows that I must wipe,
I'm just gonna be a lazy bloke,
No work will be done; I'm going on strike.

'Till then, I'll go for car rides all day,
'Till then, I'm keeping all of my pay,
'Till then, I'm gonna have all the say,
My dear — 'till then.

Welcome home my dearest one,
Living alone is not much fun,
The house was so quiet; I missed you dear,
And I cried each night in my glass of beer.

Dad and Dave are feeling glum,
There's rumblings deep down in our tum,
We need our Mum at home to lead us,
So, get well soon - come back and feed us.

(We've run out of baked beans you see.)

AN ODE FOR RECOVERY
(written by son David)

The Cooke house scene is all aghast,
Oh, Mother dear don't let it last,
The housework being done by men,
Demands the return of Mum again.

So as you relax and enjoy your stay,
In hospital as you lay,
Just think of us, all on our own,
Hoping you get better and hurry home.

IS A PUZZLEMENT!

Whilst performing all the household chores,
I had to take a little pause,
To write a little welcome ode,
On your safe return to the Cooke abode .

Welcome back my little one,
I think you find the work all done,
Although, in keeping with the past,
I had to move a trifle fast.

To Guy's you went with a dodgy back,
Now, there's one thing I must know,
Why on earth, then, did they hack,
A bit more off your toe?

WELCOME HOME – ER DARLING

She's coming home again,
delighted that's quite plain.

I've missed her sitting in her chair,
Missed her footstep on the stair.

In Loving Memory

The welcome home - the cheery smile,
The kiss that makes the day worthwhile,
She's been away a short time only,
But goodness! how the house seems lonely.

Now soon she'll be at home once more,
I guess I'd better clean the floor,
And afterwards, I think,
I'll wash the dishes in the sink.

And, heavens! there's the beds to make,
And washing too, for goodness sake,
The fridge is bare, the pantry's nude,
And a mouse has died for lack of food.

Then the garden looks a sight,
So much so, the other night,
I had to climb the apple tree,
To find out where the dog could be.

The grass stood tall, three feet or more,
And she couldn't find the kitchen door,
so, there's grass to cut - as well,
As many a jungle plant to fell.

There's polishing and things galore,
Which must be done, and then some more,
So extra time I'll have to seek,
Darling - can you stay another week?
Aug. 19th 1970.

GET WELL SOON - YOU 'ORRIBLE LITTLE PATIENT YOU

Get well soon my little one,
Sorry you've been so sad and glum,
I hope it's all been worth the while,
And soon that frown becomes a smile.

Come home soon, I love you only,
The house is cold and I'm so lonely,
It's quiet, not a sound is heard,
And I end up talking to the bird.

I've kept the kitchen clean and neat,
I've left the bathroom smelling sweet,
And on Sunday morn I really must,
Do battle with the gathering dust.

I'm free at night to visit the pub,
But, aye my dear, here's the rub,
I find to my great consternation,
I haven't the cash or inclination.

So get well soon my darling wife,
And bring the joy back to my life,
Return the warmth you took away,
And restore the sunshine to my day.
Oct 8th 1982'

MISS YOU

Come home soon my little spouse,
I miss you so about the house,
Believe me dear, from dusk till dawn,
The nights are just one great big yawn.

I find it's only half a life,
When I'm without my little wife,
So get well soon, I miss you sweet,
Come home and make my life complete.

MISSING YOU

When you go away my love,
The days are long and boring,
Outside the sun might shine above,
But inside - it is pouring.

Blackie prowls about all day,
She knows not what to do,
She's just a dog and cannot say,
How much she misses you.

Your empty bed and empty chair,
Accentuate your absence,
Your knick—knacks dotted here and there,
Do much the same in essence.

The wind howls in the chimney stack,
And silence reigns supreme,
I'm only half a man, alack,
When you're not on the scene.

So hurry home to hound and me,
And banish all this gloom,
Complete the household trinity,
And brighten every room.
(July 5th 1977)

ODE TO ONE WITH LARYNGITIS

Poor Vicki's gone and lost her voice,
And silence reigns supreme,
But I think if I had half a choice,
I'd prefer to hear her scream.

For now she talks in squeaks and rasps,
Or whispers every word,
At times she gives up with a gasp,
And whistles like a bird.

Poor girl, where are those dulcet tones?
Annunciated sharp and clear,
Words I hear with inward groans,
When I fancy half a pint of beer.

'I suppose you're going out again,
You leave me every night,
But I'd rather have her shout again,
Than see her in this plight.

So until that great day comes along,
To spare you pain and sighs,
To paraphrase that grand old song,
Speak to me only with thine eyes.
(July 13th 1978)

TO VICKI

Vicki's wild with our Barrie,
He's in the dog house alright,
She thinks he aughter,
Drink more water,
Instead of a pint each night.

But Barrie's wise to our Vicki,
She's only jealous you see ,
For While she' s taking those tablets.
She has to stay home,
Never more to roam,
Drinking gallons of tea.

Vulnerable and shy is she,
Introspective in society,
Cute and cuddly as can be,
Knows my faults and loves me still,
I love her too and always will.

I 'm just a slave, that's what I am,
Pestered by this child of Pan,
'Bring me coffee, fill my bottle,'
I swear, one day, this imp I'll throttle.

But when she sits upon my knee,
And cuddles up so close to me,
I'd rather be her slave than own,
A harem of my very own.

TO DAVID AND JILL ON THEIR WEDDING DAY

Just a wish that you may dwell,
In happiness and joy for ever,
Live each day, and live it well,
Love each moment spent together,
Always trust and help each other,
Never quarrel as the sun descends,
Drawing strength from one another,
Deepening love on this depends.
And though to end I'm very lothe,
Virtually my time is spent,
In conclusion, then, I wish you both,
Domestic bliss and sweet content.

SOME MORE VALENTINE POEMS

'Cos Valentines are so expensive,
Here I sit, alone and pensive,
Without a card, and trying hard,
To emulate the famous bard.

I've tried roses red and violets blue,
And moon and June and you and true,
But the only phrase that sounds sincere,
Are the simple words, 'I love you dear,'
So, make my day - say you'll be mine,
And be my darling Valentine.

I love you - you love me,
I know this for a fact,
But, today, I'd like you to agree,
To form a little pact.

I promise you, with hand on heart,
I'll be your Valentine,
If you will promise, on your part,

That you too will be mine.

ODES TO MUM'S MATHS

If only we had known before,
We'd send someone up to your door,
To help, assist, and make correct,
Until your maths were so perfect.

We've sixteen hands and sixteen feet,
To help you with this enormous feat,
So, if you're stuck and on the rocks,
Call on us — we'll wash your socks.
(Anon at Freemans).

I trust you will forgive this once,
My wife who's really quite a dunce,
At addition and, much worse, subtraction,
She's driven strong men to distraction.

She's never learned to solve square roots,
But, by devious and torturous routes,
She'll get a total from a list of figures,
With the aid of all her toes and fingers.

I've tried my best to teach my mate,
That three and three make six, not eight
But she merely smiles and nods her head,
Adds two and two and makes five instead.

At counting sheep she seems quite bright,
And always gets the total right,
She says, 'To reach the final score,
I count their legs and divide by four.

So please forgive my erring spouse,
Who's very good about the house,
As wife and Mum she has no peer,
But, I must admit, her maths are queer.

(To the ladies at the Abbey National, Gravesend. Jan. 1982)

We thank you for your little verse,
We do have customers much worse,
Variety is the spice of life they say,
All sorts of people come our way,
Your wife's adding may not be quite right,
But, at least, she's always most polite.
(From the ladies at the Abbey National in response to the above)

Thanks for the Memory,
Of strolls in Regents Park,
Kisses after dark,
Rowing trips and burning lips, that left the scarlet mark,
How lovely it was.

Thanks for the Memory,
Of dinner dance at eight,
Learning how to skate,

In Loving Memory

Movie shows and lamplight glows, and staying up 'till late,
How lovely it was.

Many's the times I told you,
I love you my darling so much,
And, oh, it was heaven to hold you,
In my arms while we danced to an air of romance.

So, thanks for the Memory,
Every moment spent with you,
Was heaven through and through,
I'm very grateful darling for happiness so true,
Thinking of you always when I'm away from you,
And thank you so much.

CHRISTMAS AND NEW YEAR

Oh Vicki, dear Vicki, the season's here again,
Of Christmas trees and fairy lights and frosty window panes,
Of happy folks and family jokes and parties on the hearth,
Of children singing carols, and snow upon the path.

The holly and the mistletoe, the tinsel and the braid,
On specially cleared mantelshelves the Christmas cards arrayed,
The bar's well stocked, the larder's full, the goodies all on view,
A season of togetherness, with friends both old and new.

Happy, joyful Christmastide, how eagerly we wait,
The atmosphere of peace and love your season will create,
And so this message comes to you, time honored and sincere,
Have a Merry Christmas and a prosperous New Year.

I know that Christmas is a time of giving,
Good food, good times and gracious living,
But this one's gone beyond a joke,
The bank is drained, I'm bust, I'm broke.

And it's all because this wife of mine,
Thinks I own a diamond mine,

Not content with gifts galore,
She has one more surprise in store.

'It's gone, she wails, 'It's up the spout,
Something I cannot do without,'
'Well get another,' says I, ' I'm not that mean,'
But, woe is me, it's the washing machine.

'No way,' says I, 'It costs too much,'
But sweetly smiles my dear old dutch,
I know you'll relent - you couldn't resent,
If you called it my Christmas present.'
(Christmas 1981)

THE MUSIC CENTRE

I don't know why I do it,
I guess I am to blame,
Then the day comes when rue it,
It's always been the same.

For months I've seen it coming,
Hints drooped like kitchen sinks,
The very air's been humming,
With sighs and nods and winks.

'All those records standing idle,'
There's a sob in every word,
Do I laugh or do I bridle,
Or pretend I haven't heard?

I ignore this subtle shakedown,
Of this persistent, sweet tormentor,
'Till the day come when I break down,
And she gets her music center.

EASTER POEMS

Dear Mum and Dad, this Easter's been,
A truly lovely one,
We've all enjoyed ourselves so much,
It's just been full of fun.

But now our weekend's over,
And back home we must go,
But you two must remember,
That we four love you so.
(Written by Jackie 5th April 1980)

At Easter we commemorate,
That long ago and fateful date,
When Jesus on his cross of pain,
Died that we might live again.

DAD!!

Here's a little ditty,
To welcome you back home,
We hope you had a lovely time,
But don't forget to phone.

Mum would love to hear from you,
She's missed you such a lot,
But when she knows it's you she hears,
She'll say, 'You are a clot!

'Who forgot his suit?' she'll say,
'You left it in the hall,
If it wasn't for me, you know,
You'd have probably left it all.

(Written by Jackie. August 1981)

Well, well, look who's here,
Welcome home Daddy dear,
We hope you have a happy day,
In every sort of little way.

(A happy welcome from, Grahame, Chris, Mummy and David)

THE WASHING UP BLUES

The only thing about a nosh-up,
Is, after it you have to wash up,
Plates and dishes we can eat,
Would make my happiness complete.

Pots and pans and cups galore,
All I see is more and more,
Ne'er a day is passed without,
'Washing up,' I hear them shout.

Never mind, Dad,
If it wasn't for you,
We'd all be here,
Washing too.

(Written by Dad and Jackie, Xmas 1979)

ANOTHER WELCOME HOME

You've only been away a day,
But, welcome home, dear, anyway,
I see you've lost a bit of fat,
I bet you're pleased as punch at that.
(Written by Barrie. Nov. 12th 1981)

LYNETTE

Lynette, she's quite a pet,
With eyes of blue and flaxen hair and skin so fair,
She's the picture of innocence.
But looks belie, she's not so shy,

To give you my opinion, she's a pupil of St. Trinian,
She's a bundle of mischief,
Hates men, she's only ten,
When we take the dog for walks,
She jabbers, chatters, talks,
She questions - I answer.
Lynnete, she's at that age,

When life is full of queries, she never, ever wearies of asking questions.
We went to Dover - looked the place over,
The castle keep, the turrets tall, we saw them all,
Then on to the beach,
Lynette - got very wet,
The sun was out, the tide was in,
And in she jumped with a great big grin,
Displacing volumes of water.

A day of sun, a day of fun,
She left her mark that week she stayed,
And I'm very much afraid,
She'll have to come again.

NATURE

What is nature?
Is it the trees and the plants,
Or the oceans and seas,
Or even the birds and animals and bees?

Could it be the climate, the rain and the clouds?
Perhaps even knowledge of the and stars.
The insects are nature, the pretty birds too ,
Birds like the starling, the robin and the cuckoo.
(Written by Christopher)

TO MUM AND DAD COOKE WITH LOVE

Too often it appears that your children have gone,
They 're all up and grown, your teaching is done,
But do they remember how hard you have tried,
How much you have missed them, and how you have cried?

Though many a year has just passed you by,
With no thought for yourselves as the years quickly fly,
I'd like to belong, for I know that you care,
And when you're in trouble, you know I'll be there,
And when we are married with children our own,
We know that we'll welcome you into our home,
Our lives will be busy with loving and caring,
But deep down inside, it's our love we'll be sharing,
So I hope that you'll take this message of mine,
And share it with me in the loneliest times,
For I'll love you and give all the love in my heart,
To my parents-to-be when our thoughts are apart.

(Written by Linda, a girl friend of Christopher's)

TO A VERY SPECIAL GRANDMOTHER

The lights went out, quick and fast,
I was only thinking of the past,
The moon shone through the window pane,
I heard a shout from the lane,
It was only the howling of the mut,
That explained the crying, but,
The lights went out because of a power cut.

(I love you Nanny. I'll always be there for you. Mark)

Our dearest Granddad, I do love you,
perhaps the time has come for me to make a brew,
Every time I see you, you look so well,
Relax, please, when you leave that hospital,
Another operation will come soon,
I'm giving Nan a chance to use her broom,

In case you wondered how Nanny was,
Our day in Kings Lynn was exciting 'cause,
Nanny could Just not pause,
So I got an early treat from a pretend Santa Claus.

*(To Grandad. You've always been my favorite Grandad.
That day in Hyde Park is always with me. Mark.)*

ANNA
(From my novel, From Out Of The Past'.)

I see her crouching in the night,
My Anna of a thousand dreams,
Her blue eyes wide with shock and fright,
Hiding from the Searcher's beams.

I see her hand in hand with me,
Running through the silver sand,
Or gazing on a moonlit sea,
That girths a wild, primeval land.

I feel her softness in my arms,
Her moist lips pressed to mine,
While the breeze that whispers through the palms,
Carries the scent of earth and brine.

I see her 'midst the snow-capped peaks,
Her arms reach out in vain,
The tears coursing down her cheeks,
Rend my heart with grief and pain.

I hear her calling out my name,
Through the mists of time and space,
And hope burns like a living flame ,
I'll see once more that cherished face.

Keep calling Anna, loud and clear,
We have you now, it's done at last,
Soon we'll be together, dear,
In that long ago and distant past.

THE NAUGHTY THIRTY SIX (1945)

'Twas at nineteen Royal Crescent,
In the year of 'forty five,
You came home on a 'thirty six,'
It was good to be alive.

At Feltwell you had lots of these,
The camp was near at hand,
But this one differed from the rest,
It fairly beat the band.

'Twas the eleventh day of the year's first month,
If my memory serves me right,
We'd had a rather hectic day,
And got ourselves quite tight.

I couldn't see you wander home,
To the White House in that state,
So I said, 'My Mother's working nights,'
Besides it's getting late.

I said it was a pity,
To waste a comfy bed,
My conscience wouldn't let me sleep,
'Twould be like wasting bread.

To this you readily agreed,
And forthwith home we went,
Planning on a good night's sleep,
For the hectic day we'd spent.

I lent you my pyjamas,
Said, 'Tie that string up tight,
Or the trousers will become detached,
In the middle of the night.

'I'll give you time to get undressed,
And get into your bed,
Then I'll come and say goodnight,
With a little kiss,' I said.

I gave you time to get undressed,
Then knocked upon your door,
I had my kiss, half rose to go,
And then came back for more.

I said, 'It's rather cold out here,
You look so cosy there,
You said,' I dare you, come inside,
And never turned a hair.

At first I thought, 'She's joking,
But then when treble dared,
I popped inside the bedclothes,
You weren't the least bit scared.

Nestling up so close to you,
I think I went to sleep,
When I think of all that wasted time,
It darned near make me weep.

But did I go to sleep that night?
And this one's worth a quid,
Did you tie that string up tight?
I wonder if you did.

FATHER'S LAMENT

What a mess, what a fuss,
I wonder what's come over us,
Dishes piled up in the sink,
Feel like jumping in the drink.

Clothes with holes in all around,
Dust and feathers on the ground,
Window's dirty, can't see through 'em
Haven't the energy to do 'em.

Cobwebs hanging on the wall,
Muddy footprints in the hall,
Socks get up and walk away ,
Oh well, guess they'll come back home someday.

Daddy's getting very thin,
In fact there's not much left of him,
If he had a bath it is quite plain,
He'd disappear down the drain.

Stay in bed until high noon,
Guess I'll have to get up soon,
Pangs of hunger in my tummy,
David cries, 'I want my Mummy.'

So hurry home and please take charge,
Or one thing's certain, by and large,
Daddy will go up the pole,
And they'll put him in a six foot hole.
(June 1954)

MISSING YOU

That velvet curtain falls again,
Heralding the approach of night,
The stars appear one by one,
Bathing all in spiritual light.

The moon, a crescent riding high,
Coursing through the blue,
How lucky is that moon,
He's looking down on you.

Gazing at that moon,
So lonely in that vast terrain,
Seems to bring me comfort,
I too feel just the same.

I miss you so each night time,
I can't explain just why,
Pensive, I lay down on my bed,
Just gazing at the sky.

Maybe I recall those times,
When together, you and I,
So often walked and talked and kissed,
Beneath that starry sky.

It's quiet, oh so very quiet,
As I lay here with my dreams,
Earthly sounds have passed away,
The room is full of scenes.

Scenes of memories I hold so dear,
I live them all again,
I hear your voice - your laughter clear,
Ringing in my brain.

When dawn appears they fade away,
Life goes on just the same,
But I know, as soon as night draws nigh,
I'll miss you so again.
(November 1947)

ALONE

Alone, at last I can fulfil my heart's desire,
No shrill voice to tell me, 'Put out that fire!
Haven't had a wash now since, can't remember when,
No letters have I written: I've hidden the darned pen.

Alone, no back—scratching episodes mar my slumbers,
Alone, the dishes pile up in fantastic numbers,
I stay in bed 'till late now, my socks remain unsewn,
Alone, Oh isn't it heaven to be alone.
(December 27th 1952)

ODE TO THE LOSS OF YOUTHFUL VIGOUR

Two Chelsea pensioners sitting on a park bench,
Under the shade of an old willow tree,
Recalling the maidens, the English and French,
Who had donated their maidenheads free.

'Ah, those were the days, sighs one to the, other,
My prowess was known from Dunkirk to Dundee,
I remember they called me the Tripartite Lover,
'Cos each night I pleasured not one, two but three.

'Same here,' said his friend as he shook his grey locks,
'I 'd be there at the drop of a hat,
Then I got me a dose of that rotten old pox,
And I thought, that's put paid to all that.

But I never say die, so I went to the doc,
And informed him of my sorry plight,
Right there on his desk I slapped me old cock,
And said, 'Get that ready by Saturday night.

'But now things are different, and it's not my grey hairs,
'Cos it's only happened of late,
Why, only last week, I chased up the stairs,
Mrs Price the caretaker's mate.

His comrade concurred with many a sigh,
Then two shapely girls passed the pair,
They were followed by two pairs of lack—lustre eyes,
And not a hint of a glint gleamed in there.

Then slowly the eye of one- closed in a wink,
'I've got it,' he said with a smirk,
Remember that bromide they put in our drink?
Well I think it's beginning to work.

MOTHER'S DAY POEM FROM MARK TO HIS MUM

This is a special message to a Mum that is mine,
To say I love her and hope her Mother's Day is fine,
To tell her I love her very much,
I hope to God we never loose touch.

A special gift to this lady I refer,
Not Frankincense, gold or Myrrh,
But to tell her my love truly I give,
For ever and ever, as long as she lives.

I really hope you have a wonderful day,
To tell you I love you, I don't have to say.
(Sunday, March 26th 1995)

NAN

For a Nan that is a gem - not a diamond or a ruby,
But a wonderful lady whom I do love so dearly,
A lady that has been with me through thick and thin,
A woman who I look at that makes me grin,
Her sense of humour is a wonderful thing,
I tell myself off - I don't often ring,
I hope this poem reaches you fine,
For my last chance to tell you,
That you are truly mine.

(Written by Mark April 1995)

LIFE SOMETIMES

Times are changing, times are sad,
Not all the people in this world are bad,
Many people with ambitions and success,
Even through Drama, trauma and stress,
People around me care so much,
But I find it hard to keep in touch,
With the ever changing world of now.
Many people shouting aloud,
Their cries for help are not justly seen,
But here are acts of scaredness they don't really mean.
Some people have ups and downs,
Some just mess around like clowns,
They deal with their problems in different ways,
Some find the right path and some go astray,
But this is good and not so bad,
So lighten up and don't be sad.
(Written by Mark April 1995)

The Easter Bunny and hot-cross buns,
Hope Easter Sunday brings some fun,
With treasure thrills and chocolate eggs,
I'd rather have a Yorkie egg.
But my wish is that you and Grandad are fine ,
On this special day at Easter time.
(Written by Mark April 1995)

A SAD/GLAD STORY

Oh, where's my little 'black bonce' gorn?
Here I sit and gaze forlorn,
At pictures taken in her prime,
As she was, once upon a time.

Dark and lustrous was her hair,
With little wavelets here and there,
Tumbling in abundant mass,
The crowning glory of our lass.

Then, suddenly, there came a day,
When the first long strand of grey,
Appeared in the mirror's bright reflection,
A blemish marring dark perfection.

In Loving Memory

Horrified she plucked it out,
And, for a while, there is no doubt,
Her hair retained its former glory,
But that's not the end of our sad/glad story.

For, like a grim, remorseless foe,
The streaks of grey began to show,
And the fight continued day by day,
To keep the creeping blight at bay.

Rinses, colours, washes, sets,
All theses things were tried, and yet,
Underneath those darkened tresses,
Lay what anybody's guess is.

So, tired of this futile fight,
She resolved, one day, that come what might,
She'd tackle the problem at its source,
And then let nature take its course.

So as the weeks and months went by,
Gradually grey replaced the dye,
And then, right where the grey had been,
Her hair became a silver sheen.

Though now 'black bonce' has gone for ever,
And dark—haired memories leave me never,
When silver tresses crown her head,
My 'silver bonce' is there instead.
(April 1995)

FROM FRANK TO MONICA ON THEIR 50th ANNINERSARY

A Czech from the border with Poland,
Came to the East Anglian lowland,
To find the girl of his heart,
Far from his home in 'forty three,
After fighting to keep the world free.
They met and the swore not to part.

But they couldn't be one,
'Till the war had been won,
And in 'forty five they were married.
Then came the years,
Of the joy and the tears,
And the burdens that each one had carried.
Through fine and foul weather,
They've now been together,
Married fifty years of their life,
And for those years that were spent,
In love and content,
I give thanks to my wonderful wife.
(May 14th 1995)

A POEM FROM ME TO YOU

G is for generous, you outshine the rest,
R is for remembering our times were the best,
A is for always my thoughts are with you,
N is for no way, could there be anyone to replace you two,
D is for directions you've tried to show me,
P is for pleasant, it rubs off on us you see,
A is for awkward I know I've been in the past,
R is for rascal, of that you've seen the last.
E is for everlasting, your love will live on,
N is for never, I wont leave contact for long,
T is for togetherness, that's the Cooke family way,
S is for simply, my love will not stray.

(Love Mark – Received 13/6/97)

DISILLUSION

I long to see my home again, the place of my birth bids me return,
And, oh the sweet, nostalgic pain, consumes my heart with a fierce burn.

To see the old familiar faces, to see the house where I was born,
To see the well remembered faces; the sunrise tint the hills at dawn.

I went to see my town again, and stood outside the station,
I felt my heart restrict with pain as I viewed the devastation.

A motorway had slashed its way, through the urban conurbation,
Where first I saw the light of day, was now a filling station.

The hills that once stood fresh and green, now were brown and dry,
Where farms and cottages once had been, pylons march across the sky.

Obscene graffiti here and there, tatty posters, peeling paint,
The 'dozers clatter everywhere, destroying all that's old and quaint.

The leafy lanes where once we strayed, are steel and concrete caverns,
On golden sands where once we played; a sprawling fair and taverns.

Shops and houses old in time, razed to build a superstore,
Factories pour forth smoke and grime; a steelworks stands hard by the shore.

I sought the well remembered faces, but they were strangers now to me,
Age and infirmity now replace, the fresh-faced youths they used to be.

I'd come, I'd seen but, oh my dears, my heartaches still abide,
It breaks for all those long, lost years, and a town that lost its pride.

A VALENTINE POEM. FEB. 14th 1996

Upon this day eponymous,
The Valentine must be anonymous,
So the written word must be the animus ,
To convey his thoughts of love most amorous.

A VALENTINE POEM FEB 14th 1997

A Valentine card cannot express,
The thrill of a kiss, a soft caress,
But words composed by a swain can bring,
The very next best to the real thing.

So, please accept these words sincere,
From one whose love grows year by year,
And never allow a rhyme by others,
To speak the private words of lovers.

TO MUM AND DAD

It's nice to find a present,
When you open your front door,
You read the words that's written,
And wonder what's in store.

It's two blue shirts for Dad,
And something nice to eat,
I wonder if you've guessed by now,
It's Army and Navy sweets.

There's also a little present,
Addressed especially to Mum,
It might be some confectionery,
Or even chewing gum.

I tried to get your favorite,
I looked round high and low,
But the shops in Bampton village,
Don't sell your Jellio!

So I had to settle for second best,
You know it was such a plight,
But I'm sure you're just as pleased as me,
To have a bar of Turkish Delight.

Love from
Grahame and Jackie
Mark and David

(Written around Xmas 1981)

FOR EVE AND ON THEIR FIFTIETH WEDDING ANNIVERSARY

Marriages are made in heaven,
Especially those of forty seven,
Fifty years have slipped away,
Enjoy your Golden Wedding Day
(November 29th 1997)

I had a little run, then I had a little pain,
So I had a little brandy to numb my little brain,
I numbed my little brain, then collapsed upon the floor,
And now I •have a bigger pain than the one I had before.
(Inspired by Vicki trying to run — June 1998)

Mothers' Day Poem from Mark to his Mum
(Sunday, 26th March 1995)

This is a special message to a Mum that's mine,
To say I love her and hope her Mothers' Day is fine,
To tell her I love her very much,
I hope to God we never loose touch.

A special gift to this lady I refer,
Not Frankincense, gold or myrrh,
But to tell her my love I truly give,
Forever and ever as long as she lives.

I really hope you have a wonderful day,
To tell you I love you I don't have to say!

FLO AND "L 'S FORTIETH WEDDING ANNIVERSARY

When Vera sang "We'll meet again,"
And bombs fell from the sky like rain,
When labeled children left by train,
Flo and Wal got married.

When wardens yelled, "Put out that light!"
And sirens wailed by day and night,
When we braced ourselves for the coming fight,
Flo and Wal got spliced.

When contrails scarred the summer sky,
And gas masks slapped against each thigh,
When every stranger was a spy,
Flo and Wal got hitched.

When a soldier's pay was a bob a day,
And rationing was here to stay,
When Gable, Wayne and Flynn held sway,
Flo and Wal got shackled.

When, each night, people could be found,
Trooping down the Underground,
When a pound was really worth a pound,
Flo and Wal were wedded.

When Churchill cheered our finest hours,
And people planted veg. not flowers,
When we fought to defend this land of ours,
Flo and Wal got knotted.

Shortly after they were matched,
Wal was hastily dispatched,
To Greece and told to keep the peace,
But Jerry put him in the bag. (poor Flo).

And after five long years inside,
Wal returned to his brand new bride,
Then, hand in hand and side by side,
They bravely faced the future.

In Loving Memory

And now we celebrate that day,
Just forty years ago,
When Jerry basked in the Rue de Ia Pais,
And Wally Married Flo.

ST. VALENTINE'S DAY 2000

My Valentine is always there,
To hold my hand, to stroke my hair,
My Valentine's the one I love,
My heart, my soul, all else above.

My Valentine's a lovely smile,
That makes it all seem worth the while,
My Valentine is good and true,
My Valentine, my love, is you.

ST.VALENTINE'S DAY 2001

Today I give these words to you,
In tenderness and love so true,
Read them and place them in your heart,
And recall them when you're feeling blue.

The above refers to words on the Valentine card.

DAVID LEFT HIS RAZOR BEHIND

Thank you for your welcome gift,
To see it gave me quite a lift,
But I must return this razor fine,
'Cos you see, it isn't really mine.

ANOTHER VALENTINE POEM

Nothing ever stays the same,
But one thing I know fine,
No matter what else changes,
You'll always be my Valentine.

A LIMERICK

So, Osama Bin Laden,
For you there can be no pardon,
We'll catch the creep,
And bury him deep,
In a plot at the foot of my garden.

Sent to the Daily Mail on 15/10/01

ANOTHER VALENTINE POEM

What can I say?
My love grows more for you each day,
And now I express my love my way,
With a Valentine card for you this day.

St Valentine's day 2002

OH, WHAT A SCANDAL

Oh, what a scandal,
I've broken a handle,
And a couple of tea cups as well,
When I told the wife,
She gave me some strife,
And told me I should go to hell.
But, I apologised most contritely,
And I guess I got off quite lightly.
So, in future I'd better beware,
And handle such things with great care,

'Cos if I don't I reckon there'll be,
A place in the garage for me.

Written on November 15th 2004

OBSERVING THE TYE

Through this window for half a decade,
I've looked on the Tye and new plans made,
I've scribbled thoughts that turned into rhymes,
On life now and how it was in old times.

Look! a man and his dog on the Tye,
Later a horse and rider canters by,
But now all seems quiet and very still,
So my mind and pen do as they will.

The Tye has changed little through the years,
But different scenes each day appears,
Some days cows graze and chew the cud,
Summertime mushrooms grow in the mud.

Bank holiday, Telcombe village, the Target,
A beautiful sight so many eyes met,
Daffodils dancing gaily in the sun,
Satisfying to the mind; a feast for everyone.

Happiness one can gain, happiness one can renew,
Unobtainable by the many, gained by the few,
Moon, sun stars, rivers, the ever changing sea,
Birds, plants, trees; all this brings happiness to me.

*(Written by Nan Ramsey and read by
her daughter at her funeral 6/10/96)*

BLESSINGS

What blessings a child born out of wedlock can bring,
After the storms of life I can sing,

Blessings, blessings more and more,
Grandchildren coming through the door.

The pleasure and love from a grandson's kiss,
Is heaven on earth and pure bliss.
So, my child, thank you for all you have given me,
Through you and yours I have found the key ,
To true happiness and joy of living.

(Written by Nan Ramsey)

MY LIFE

I really was an awful dope,
When with that man I did elope,
It gave my parents so much pain,
Yet I feel I would do the same, if I had my life again.

I was selfish, mean and gay,
But I never had to pay,
Lovers came thick and fast,
Never minding my lurid past.

Then the war and dear, true Alex,
Now life became serious and complex,
Bombs dropped from the skies,
perhaps all that suffering made me wise.

We stayed together many a year,
Then we married - it was only fair,
He had proved himself good, brave and true,
With him I never could be through.

MY GRANDSONS

Very proud I am of my grandsons three,
Fine men they are going to be,
David plays rugby, gets tries but gets hurt,

Chris is a runner, determined to get first.

Grahame the youngest is and gay,
Adventures galore will come his way,
Vicki, my daughter and Barrie my son—in—law,
Have treated me well and cannot do more..

When they have grandchildren,
And think of the past,
I hope, like me, they will say,
Life has been good, but has gone too fast.

MY EIGHTEENTH BIRTHDAY

My eighteenth birthday, a night of romance,
A love-sick girl, a love-sick boy in a trance.

Life brings forth both losses and gains,
The tears are forgiven, the music remains.

Although countless days have come and gone,
I can 'till hear echoes of that lovely song.

THOUGHTS ON A LOVELY DAUGHTER

A letter from Vicki to start the day,
Her joys she does not have far to seek,
Letters and visits from her sons so dear,
Fill her weeks with love and good cheer.

She is a simple, dear good woman,
Sharing her life with a dear, good man,
May their lives go on filled with simple joys,
As the years go by, grandchildren, girls and boys .
Written on 29th February 1972

EDIE (1907 - 1970)

At one I was my Mother's pride and joy,
At fifteen I was in love with my first boy,
At eighteen I had my daughter dear,
This made me leave home, woeful and with many tears.

At twenty five I married a man named John,
In the Isle of wight while living with my sister Con,
While Hitler was in power I was in love with Tony,
When war broke out, he left me sad and lonely.

Now I am old and sixty three,
I'm as happy as a woman should be,
Living in Saltdean with the first and last love of my life,
Thanking the powers that be for making me his wife.

LOOKING BACK

Looking back to April fifteenth nineteen thirty three,
My first marriage took place to John Beattie,
Unsuccessful, as I was madly in love with another man.
My turn came to be deserted when World War Two began.
Then, what was proved to be the best and last love, entered my life,
And life became worthwhile, when I became a true, loving wife.

(Written 15/4/1981)

A COMFORT TO BOTH MUM AND DAD

Vicki and Barrie Cooke, thirty one years wed,
For this marriage there's a lot to be said.
Overcoming the many tribulations and cares,
Two devoted and happy people throughout the years,

A comfort to both parents Mother and Dad.
Thinking back, we two feel happy and glad,
That wartime romance proved lasting and true.

Here's wishing many more 'Happy Anniversaries' to you.

YESTERDAY'S RUGBY MATCH

These rhymes I compose are mostly atrocious,
Should I desist, become sane and cautious?
Write letters more often to friends and relations,
Give up functions and my foolish pretensions.

It would be rather sad if I say farewell,
While I still have many a tale to tell.
For instance, chosen to play for England, David Cooke,
Television switched on, our books quickly forsook.

A good game, but alas our side lost,
Nine points to twenty four Wales won at a cost.
Many players bruised and battered, Rugby's rough,
The men of Rugby have to be strong and tough.

TO VICKI AND BARRIE ON THEIR 25th WEDDING ANNIVERSARY

To two dear people we send this card,
With much love and great regard,
Grandsons now full grown men, a credit to your loving care,
How happy and proud your Mum and Dad are to share,
This twenty fifth anniversary of that wonderful day,
Which, somehow, does not seem all that far away,
The Kensington Registry Office, the Cumberland Hotel,
The photographers; these memories! All's well that ends well.

DAVID COOKE

Thirty two! The years of rugby over and done,
Plenty of admiration he has deservedly won,
He'll have more time now with Jill and his small son.

He'll miss the glory, those comradely times,
But he's not the type of chap who whines,
And he'll have those memories of bygone times.

TWENTY THREE ON THE TENTH

A rhyme to David Alexander Cooke,
A teacher, a man of good looks,
He plays rugby and never cowers,
Seldom do we see this grandson of ours.

We think and feel he's a bachelor gay,
But he will not always be that way,
We had our days in the sun,
He's entitled to his youth and fun.

One day he'll procure a wife,
With luck we two will have long life,
Just thinking this gives us a thrill,
A child, nursery rhymes, Jack and Jill,
Time and our lives are hurrying by,
So this could happen in the twinkling of an eye,
Grandparents at forty one and forty three respectively,
To obtain great grandparent-ship, what joy this would be.

A NEW GENERATION

Chris engaged to a girl named Lynne,
So once more the old, old story begins,
Love, marriage, offspring in sight,
Grandma and Grandpa filled with delight.

The pride and pleasure in a new generation,
These thoughts filling us with a new elation,
So please Father time, give us the time to enjoy,
More of the seeds sowed when we were girl and boy.

In love with love, our youth went quickly by,
But now together for ever and ever until we die,
A complicated and unusual life we both led,

In Loving Memory

Our daughter 'a treasure' can be said and re-said.

NEXT DAY CALLED – I DUST

I dust, I cook, I read, I write,
With this my life I do not fight,
The years have gone when nights were wild,
Fifty years since I gave birth to my child.

That child into a woman has grown,
She now has three sons of her own,
Two sons married, three grandsons born,
Life has many facets, we've no reason to moan.

(Written by Nan Ramsey on the occasion of Vicki's 51st birthday)

VICKI'S 47th BIRTHDAY

The twenty fourth of March again Vicki dear,
So birthday wishes for a bright new year,
May the day dawn with the sun above,
Surrounded with thoughts from the ones you love,
Troubles may come, but they wont last,
We will all love you more as the years fly past.

(Written by Nan Ramsey 24/3/1973)

VICKI'S 45th BIRTHDAY

For you a birthday rhyme,
Hoping it gets to you in time,
Have fun and joy in all you do,
Never forgetting that I am thinking of you.

Many, many happy returns of the day my love,
And loving wishes for a gay new year.

BARRIE

Our son by marriage, shortly reaching fifty one,
Three sons, three grandsons the outcome,
Of a love affair that survived the years,
'Happy ever after; the answer to my prayers.

DAVID! TWENTY NINTH BIRTHDAY

Captain of the Harlequins! Proud Mother, proud Grandmother.
A true blue Conservative Father and a Communist Grandfather,
This mixture has brought forth a fine, handsome man,
How good to see one's roots good and strong before one's race is run,
What more can one ask, to live and see the roots thriving,
Our only daughter, happily wed, into her fifty second year arriving.

CHRIS AND HIS GUITAR

Chris came with his guitar,
Do, ray, me, so, far,
He filled the room with music and song,
Carrying us back to the days we were young.
Those years we had fun and gaiety galore,
Now with this grandson were're having more.
This gay troubadour of ours,
Gave us pleasure for many hours,
Now back to his home he has gone,
The memory of his music lingers on.

Chris has left home with his guitar,
Upsetting both his Ma and Pa,
One day soon he be back again,
Until that day the echoes of his refrains,
Will cheer his folk and keep them gay,
In this world of ours, young men must go their way,
Life has been like this for centuries and more,
Sex and love will put their heads around the door.

It's all in the nature of things,
My grandson Chris is having his fling,
Try, dear boy, not to hurt the girl in the case,
When you part, don't let her lose face.
Life must be lived, and it's all experience,
But do keep and use common sense.

GRAHAME AND HIS SONS

Back to the past my mind strays,
As I think of Father and sons with loving ways,
Mark! Hazel eyes, golden hair - like his Mother,
David! Freckled, hair brightly polished copper.

First love not regretted as I relive the past,
The various stages of my life going too fast.

HAPPY BIRTHDAY ALEX

For you another birthday ditty,
It would be nice if I made it witty,
But may this day be full of love,
Hopes realised, blue skies above,
The new year's bringing new joys and blisses,
Each day ending with our good night kisses.
Sunday! Sunshine and love abounded,
Monday! Feelings slightly wounded,
Tuesday! Sir in Town and sixty seven,
Wednesday! Chicken and wine; once more in heaven,
Thursday! We must wait and see,
Friday! Also what may be,
Saturday! The rounds again,
But each week not quite the same.

(Written by Nan Ramsey on Alex's real birthday. 15/3/1905)

HAPPY OFFICIAL BIRTHDAY ALEX

Fourteenth of fifteenth, it matters not,
He was born; grew up to share my lot.
Karl Marx died in the fourteenth, years before,
But not before opening wide the door,
To revolution and rising of the people,
Who go on, seemingly, for ever climbing the steeple.
It would be something to see the end of the race,
Before we leave this weird and wonderful place.
I am one of those mixed-up kind of beings,
Not up to all these beliefs without seeing.
Since we came on this earth to dwell ,
This world has often been through hell.

(Written by Nan Ramsey on Alex's 'official' 67th birthday)

VICKI

Many happy returns dear, most dear, daughter,
March on with the years, don't let your steps falter,
Thoughtful and kind for many, many years,
Causing few troubles and very few cares.
May your day be gay, happy and joyful,
May your world get more and more peaceful,
May life go on being good for you and yours,
May you be spared from many of life's cares.

(Written by Nan Ramsey on Vicki 's birthday 24 March 1978)

TO COMMEMORATE BOBBY'S BIRTH

The baby was born on St. Michael's day,
Another human being to have his say.
Robert Barrie Cooke the name he will carry,
On this Earth long may he tarry,
Great Grandmother am I now to four,
May poverty never knock on their door,

In Loving Memory

May love and happiness come their way,
And on this Earth long may they stay.

(Written by Nan Ramsey on Bobby's birthday 1979)

VICKI'S BIRTHDAY 24th Match 1978

Fifty two years, glad and sad memories return,
Of the home that was mine when Vicki was born,
Love and kisses the good fairy provided,
These gifts Vicki has used and never derided.
Fifty two years, Father Time skipping by,
Fifty two years have flown - smother that sigh.

CHRISTOPHER'S DAY 1978

Christopher's twenty sixth birthday; one of my joys.
In this family now six loved and affectionate boys,
Three grandsons quickly grow up, reach manhood,
To see the three babes do this, I would if I could,
But this can never be, so let fancy take over,
World wide peace and plenty, no need to cower.
Our children, their children! our roots for ever thriving,
We pass away; make way for others arriving.

(by Nan Ramsey)

VICKI'S BIRTHDAY 24/3/80

Our offspring's birthday, a sunny morn,
It wasn't so the day she was born.
Fifty four years ago she reached this shore,
In a rocky boat, the Mother tragic and poor.
The years rolled on, happiness she found,
A steady man, their children around,
The Mother followed in the self-same path,
Both without riches, this aftermath.

(Written by Nan Ramsey)

BIRTHDAY POEM 24/3/1926

A child snuggles up close to a Mother's breast,
A new life has begun; forgiven the past,
A grandmother now that child has become,
All's well that ends well, booms the gun.
Helpless into life all babies are born,
All should be loved not just some,
Thinking of the uncared for brings deep resentment,
Thinking of our babies brings forth contentment.

(Written by Nan Ramsey)

A BIRTHDAY POEM TO VICKY WRITTEN OVER TWO DAYS 24/3/76

What to rhyme about; troubles taboo,
Goodbye to those days of sickness and flu,
Excitement abounds; a brand new year,
So shake off all your worries and cares, dance little lady,
As this glorious sun sparkles on the blue sea,
Our sons are bringing forth new faces,
Fifty years have flown away the traces.

From Gwen Tester July 2002

Today's a very important date,
One for all to celebrate,
For fifty five years ago you two,
Stood side by side and said "I do."

A life of love, laughter and tears,
Some joy, some sorrow, hopes and fears,
Now family and friends are here to share,
Your special blessing because we care.

We do not know what lies in store,
But, here's to quite a few years more,
So, as you now retake each oath,
Be happy and God bless you both.

From Mark 4th October 2003

It has been a while since,
A scone and tea,
When I asked my Nan,
For my money back you see.

So to take her for lunch,
And my Granddad as well,
I hope now my story,
I can sit here and tell.

That once I was not in the family way,
And nor is Julie, that is why we can't stay,
And so happy she is, but bewildered maybe,
That my Nanny and Granddad are the best there can be.

St. Valentine's day Feb. 14th 2004

You're the air I breathe, You're the beat of my heart,
I love you now as I did from the start.

THE BLESSING

How can I describe that lovely day?
So wonderful in every way,
Mum looked lovely in something blue,
Something borrowed, something new,
But the finest sight I ever saw,
Was the veiled, grey hat that Mother wore,
The guests arrived all neatly dressed,
Even Chris's pants were pressed,
We rode to the church in Grahame's car,

Beribboned as all marriage vehicles are,
Now, at the church, here we are,
In our pews waiting for the star,
The father said 'Stand for the bride,
My heart burst with pride and everyone cried,
She walked down the aisle on the arm of her son,

And we stood holding hands, together as one,
Some hymns were sung, some prayers were said,
The rings exchanged and we were wed.
Outside the church the crowd waits there,
Flashbulbs popping everywhere,
The confetti fell from the sky like rain,
Then into the car and off again.
The reception was held at the Conservative club,
Festooned with balloons and lots of grub,
The guests were all seated, a glass in their hands,
Glenn Miller was playing and other dance bands,

There was a celebratory atmosphere in the air,
And a spirit of bon by everyone there,
Grahame called for quiet and made a lovely speech,
Mum cried buckets and I coloured like a peach,
Not to be left upon the shelf,
I rose to make a speech myself,
Thanking the boys for all they've done,
To make this day a happy one,
Midst much applause, we cut the cake,
A lovely one which Tracy baked,
Lots of talk, lots of fun,
And then the entertainment's done.
Now all the guests are going home,
Leaving the happy couple all alone,
As up the path we wend our way,
And close the door on a wondrous day.

DAD

I remember long ago,
When only Mummy's Day was so,
gut now a Father's Day comes too,
And other days for me and you.

Why this Surge in special days,
For things so special and always?
Who decreed that this should be
This day for you and one for me?

I sense cold hearts with greed at play
These ones who always have the say
Their aim to make every day
A special day for which to pay …...

For cards and gifts and special ways
To give loved ones who asked no praise
Except to know that what they do
Has been the best for me and you.

Now technology steps in
To give a way to damp their gain
An email is no cost at all
To give one's love to one and all.

Though I may use their Fathers Day
To send my love to you this way
Please know one day is not enough
To send you all my love.

so every day throughout the year
Always know that I am here
To be with you should you call
To always be your son that's all.

I love you Dad, Chris

A POEM FROM DAVID

We love you very much,
even though we're out of touch,
And although we seem to be worlds apart,
This message comes from the heart,
A Happy Birthday poem for our dear Mum,
So now you can smile and not be glum.

From your son what lives in Frenchland.
Love you Mum

David xxxxxx

Grandad - 11/9/2011

It broke our hearts to lose you,
But you didn't go alone,
Apart of us went with you,
The day God took you home.

A million times we missed you,
A million times we cried,
If love could have saved you,
You never would have died.

To the grave we travel,
The flowers are placed with care,
No-one knows the heartache,
As we turn to leave you there.

If tears could build a stairway,
And heartaches could make a lane,
We would walk a path to heaven,
And bring you back again.

Christian Cooke

Printed in Poland
by Amazon Fulfillment
Poland Sp. z o.o., Wrocław